TIMELINE OF MICHELANGELO'S LIFE

1475 — Michelangelo is born in Caprese, Italy.

1488 — At age 13, Michelangelo travels to Florence, Italy, to become an apprentice in the workshop of Domenico Ghirlandaio.

1490 — Michelangelo decides he is more interested in sculpting than painting. He is invited to study sculpting at the palace of wealthy art lover Lorenzo de' Medici.

1494 — Many citizens of Florence, including Michelangelo, leave the city. They are afraid the French king, Charles VIII, and his army will attack the city. Michelangelo goes to Venice, where he is inspired by the architecture and light reflecting from Venice's canals. Then he goes to Bologna to create statues for the Church of St. Dominic.

1496 — Michelangelo is hired to create two statues in Rome. One of them is the *Pieta*.

THIS WAY

1501 — Returns to Florence, where he creates the statue of David.

1505 — Travels back to Rome to work for Pope Julius II. The Pope wanted Michelangelo to carve lots of statues to decorate his tomb, a job that would take years.

1508 — The Pope orders Michelangelo to stop carving statues and begin painting the ceiling of the Sistine Chapel.

1513 — Michelangelo returns to carving the statues for Pope Julius's tomb.

1519 — Begins work on six major statues for the Medici Chapel in Florence.

1536 — In Rome, Michelangelo begins working on a huge painting called *The Last Judgment*.

1545 — Michelangelo finally completes the tomb of Julius II.

1547 — Michelangelo designs the gigantic dome for St. Peter's Basilica.

1564 — Michelangelo dies in Rome at the age of 88.

UP HERE

GETTING TO KNOW THE WORLD'S GREATEST ARTISTS

MICHELANGELO

WRITTEN AND ILLUSTRATED BY MIKE VENEZIA

CONSULTANT MEG MOSS

CHILDREN'S PRESS®

An Imprint of Scholastic Inc.

New York Toronto London Auckland Sydney
Mexico City New Delhi Hong Kong
Danbury, Connecticut

For Jeannine

Cover: Detail, *Creation of Sun and Moon at Sistine chapel,* Vatican, Rome, Italy.
© Massimo Pizzotti/age fotostock

Library of Congress Cataloging-in-Publication Data

Venezia, Mike, author, illustrator.
  Michelangelo / by Mike Venezia.—Revised Edition.
     pages cm.—(Getting to know the world's greatest
artists)
Includes index.
  ISBN 978-0-531-21977-5 (library binding)—
ISBN 978-0-531-22538-7 (pbk.)
  1. Michelangelo Buonarroti, 1475-1564—Juvenile
literature. I. Title.

N6923.B9V44 2014
709.2—dc23
[B]   2014015029

©2015 by Mike Venezia Inc.

All rights reserved. Published in 2015 by Children's Press, an imprint of Scholastic Inc.
Printed in China 62

SCHOLASTIC, CHILDREN'S PRESS, and associated logos are trademarks and/or
registered trademarks of Scholastic Inc.

4 5 6 7 8 9 10 R 24 23 22 21 20 19 18 17 16 15

Detail of the *Bust of Michelangelo*. By Daniele da Volterra. Bronze.
Galeria della Accademia, Florence. Scala/Art Resource, New York

Michelangelo Buonarroti was born
near Florence, Italy, in 1475, during
a time known as the Renaissance.
Many people think he was the
greatest artist who ever lived.

Michelangelo was a master of architecture, painting, and poetry. But his favorite art was making statues of people.

Michelangelo sculpted many of his statues from big blocks of marble. He chipped away at the marble with a hammer and chisel, until he got it the way he liked.

The unfinished statue of *Saint Matthew* shows how Michelangelo started one of his statues.

Michelangelo made his statues look very lifelike. Sometimes he would polish them so they looked smooth and shiny.

Madonna and Child. c. 1504.
Marble, 4 feet, 2½ inches.
Church of Notre Dame, Bruges.
Scala/Art Resource, New York

Detail of
The Medici Madonna.
1524-1534. Marble,
7 feet, 5⅝ inches.
Medici Chapel in
the New Sacristy
of San Lorenzo,
Florence.
Scala/Art Resource,
New York

But sometimes Michelangelo would leave chisel marks. The marks helped give his statues shape and a feeling of being alive when they were viewed from a distance.

When Michelangelo was born his mother may have been too ill to take care of him. His father took him to live with a family of stonecutters.

When he grew up, Michelangelo joked that this was the reason he loved to cut away at stone so much.

9

Michelangelo lived in just the right place and at just the right time. In the 1400s and 1500s, people in Florence were very interested in architecture, painting, poetry, and sculpture.

When Michelangelo was 13, he learned a lot about art by just walking through the streets of Florence on his way to the school and workshop of Florence's most popular artist, Domenico Ghirlandaio.

The Ascension of St. John. By Giotto, from a fresco cycle of the Life of St. John the Evangelist. Peruzzi Chapel in Santa Croce, Florence. Scala/ Art Resource, New York

Michelangelo loved the paintings of Giotto and Masaccio that he saw on the walls of churches in Florence,

Payment of the Tribute by Christ. 1425-1428. By Masaccio, from a fresco cycle of the Life of St. Peter. Brancacci Chapel in the Church of Santa Maria del Carmine, Florence. SuperStock, New York

Left: *St. Mark.* 1411. By Donatello. Marble, 7 feet, 9 inches.
Church of Orsanmichele, Florence. Scala/Art Resource, New York

Right: *Story of Abraham.* 1425-1452. By Ghiberti, gilt bronze panels,
31¼ inches. East doors of the Florence Baptistery, right side,
2nd field, Florence. Scala/Art Resource, New York

and he admired the sculptures of
Donatello and Ghiberti. These artists
lived and worked in Florence before
Michelangelo was born.

Michelangelo learned a lot on his own, but he also learned many things about being an artist from his master, Ghirlandaio.

One important thing that Ghirlandaio may have taught Michelangelo was the difficult art of fresco painting. To make a fresco, an artist paints on wet plaster. As the plaster dries, the painting becomes part of the wall and lasts a very long time. This is because the paint won't flake off.

Fresco painting came in very handy for Michelangelo later on, when he began his most famous painting, the ceiling of the Sistine Chapel.

Michelangelo's first love was sculpture. When he was about 16, he went to study at a new school that was only for sculptors. It was started by the wealthiest and most powerful man in Florence, Lorenzo de' Medici. Lorenzo loved art of all kinds and paid artists to create works of art for him. People who paid artists in this way were known as patrons.

Lorenzo soon realized that Michelangelo had a special talent and invited him to live at his palace. The sculpture on the next page was one of the first Michelangelo did at Lorenzo's school.

Madonna of the Stairs. c. 1491.
Marble relief, 22 x 15¾ inches.
Casa Buonarroti, Florence. Scala/Art Resource, New York

Michelangelo studied as hard as he could to become a good sculptor. But it wasn't until he visited Rome that Michelangelo showed people how good he really was.

Rome was another great art city in Italy. Michelangelo made a statue for a wealthy patron there that amazed everyone who saw it.

The *Pietà* was so beautiful, people found it hard to believe it was done by such a young artist. Michelangelo was only 24.

Pietà. 1498-1499. Marble, 5 feet, 9 inches. St. Peter's Church, Vatican City, Rome, Italy

The people who ran the city of Florence heard about Michelangelo's beautiful statue. As soon as he returned home, they asked him to carve a statue for Florence. They even gave Michelangelo a huge block of marble to work with. Michelangelo was very happy. He couldn't wait to start.

It's all yours Michelangelo.

Think of it as a present.

Gee, thanks everyone!

THIS END UP

Detail of *David*. 1501-1504. Marble, 16 feet, 10 inches.
Galleria della Accademia, Florence. Scala/Art Resource, New York

Michelangelo turned the block of marble into his most famous sculpture. The statue shows David ready to fight the giant Goliath. But *David* also shows that the people of Florence thought of themselves as strong, brave, clever, and ready to defend their city.

During this time, the powerful ruler of the church in Rome heard about Michelangelo. Pope Julius II wanted to build beautiful churches and statues in Rome so that people would remember him. He asked Michelangelo to come there to work. At first, everything was fine. Pope Julius wanted Michelangelo to carve a group of statues for him. But soon after Michelangelo started, Julius lost interest in the project. He decided there was a much more important job he wanted done.

Julius asked Michelangelo to paint the large ceiling of the Sistine Chapel. Michelangelo was disappointed. He told the pope he was a sculptor, not a painter. Pope Julius didn't care what Michelangelo thought and practically forced him to begin painting. During the time it took to paint the ceiling, the pope and Michelangelo had many arguments.

Ceiling of the Sistine Chapel. 1508-1512. Vatican Palace,
Vatican City, Rome. Scala/Art Resource, New York

After four years, Michelangelo
finished the ceiling.

It turned out to be one of the most wonderful paintings in the history of art.

Creation of Adam. Detail from the Sistine Chapel ceiling.
1510. Fresco, 110 ⅛ x 224⅖ inches.
Sistine Chapel, Vatican Palace, Vatican City, Rome. Scala/Art Resource, New York

Michelangelo painted many scenes
from the Bible. One of the most famous
scenes shows God giving life to Adam.
The looks on the faces of God and
Adam and the realistic way

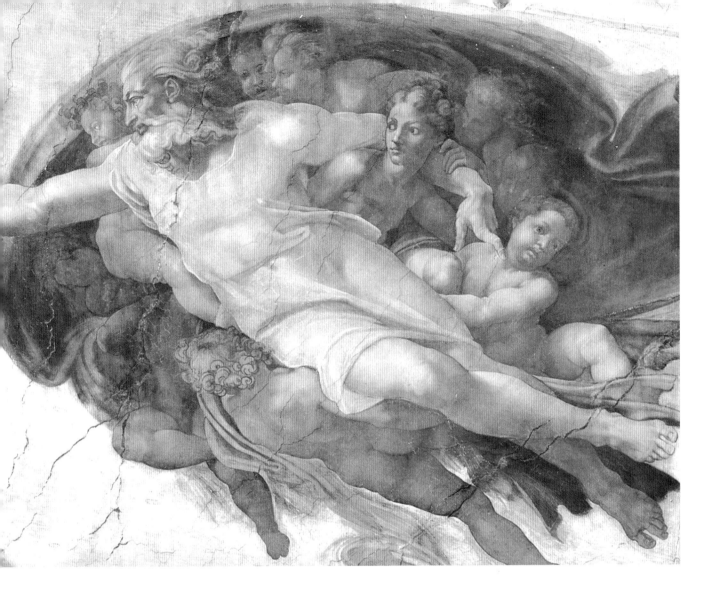

Michelangelo painted their bodies
had never been seen in a painting
before. Suddenly, Michelangelo
became known as one of the greatest
painters in the world!

Dome of St. Peter's Church, Vatican City, Rome. Gaetano Barone/SuperStock, New York

After the Sistine Chapel ceiling was finished, Michelangelo went on to create many other beautiful and important works of art, including plans for building the famous dome on top of St. Peter's Basilica in Rome.

One of the things that made Michelangelo such a great artist was his ability to give a *special* energy and strength to the people he painted and sculpted. Even though the statue of Moses is sitting very still, Michelangelo was able to give him a feeling of great power.

Moses. Detail of the Tomb of Julius II. 1506-1513. Marble, 8 feet, 4 inches. San Pietro in Vincoli, Rome. Scala/Art Resource, New York

Michelangelo lived to be nearly 89 years old. He was working on a sculpture called the *Rondanini Pietà* just a few days before he died.

Detail of *The Rondanini Pietà.*
c. 1552-1564. Marble, 6 feet, 3⅝ inches.
Castello Sforzesco, Milan.
Scala/Art Resource, New York

Below: *Creation of the Stars and Planets.*
Detail from the Sistine Chapel ceiling.
1511. Fresco, 110⅛ x 224⅞ inches.
Sistine Chapel, Vatican Palace, Vatican City, Rome.
Scala/Art Resource, New York

Michelangelo felt the human body was the most important subject an artist could paint or sculpt.

Detail of the *Last Judgment*. c. 1536-1541. Fresco, 48 x 44 feet.
Sistine Chapel (altar wall), Vatican Palace, Vatican City, Rome. Scala/Art Resource, New York

He spent much of his life studying
nature and science in order to make
his works of art as lifelike as possible.

Recently, Michelangelo's paintings in the Sistine Chapel were cleaned. When years of grime were removed, people were surprised to find that Michelangelo used much more color in his paintings than could be seen before.

The works of art in this book came from the churches and museums listed below.

Casa Buonarroti, Florence, Italy
Castello Sforzesco, Milan, Italy
Baptistery, Florence, Italy
Galleria della Accademia, Florence, Italy
Notre Dame, Bruges, Belgium
Orsanmichele, Florence, Italy
San Lorenzo, Florence, Italy
San Pietro in Vincoli, Rome, Italy
Saint Peter's Basilica, Rome, Italy
Santa Croce, Florence, Italy
Santa Maria del Carmine, Florence, Italy
Vatican Palace, Rome, Italy

LEARN MORE BY TAKING THE MICHELANGELO QUIZ!

(ANSWERS ON THE NEXT PAGE.)

1. How did Michelangelo get the 11,000-pound statue of *David* from his work shed to the city square?
- ⓐ He called a limo service.
- ⓑ He carved a giant skateboard out of marble and pushed *David* across the city.
- ⓒ He built a massive rolling wooden scaffold.

2. TRUE OR FALSE: Michelangelo invented the game of marbles when he carved little balls out of leftover marble scraps.

3. In 1504, government officials in Florence challenged Michelangelo and another famous artist to see who could paint the best battle scene. Who was the other artist?
- ⓐ Raphael
- ⓑ Leonardo da Vinci
- ⓒ Federico Fellini

4. One reason Michelangelo had a great understanding of the human body was:
- ⓐ He sketched people at the beach.
- ⓑ He dissected human corpses.
- ⓒ He took fashion-design classes.

5. When workers removed years of sticky grime from Michelangelo's Sistine Chapel ceiling, they used:
- ⓐ Chinese fish sauce and a wire brush
- ⓑ Power hoses borrowed from a local car wash
- ⓒ A special solution applied with a paintbrush and wiped off with a sponge soaked in pure water

6. What were some of Michelangelo's favorite foods?
- ⓐ Chalupas with black beans
- ⓑ Polish sausage with fries
- ⓒ Anchovies, tortellini, salami, spinach, and bread

ANSWERS

1. c The statue of *David* was carefully rolled on a giant wooden scaffold to the Piazza della Signoria, which is the town square in Florence. It took about four days to transport *David* from Michelangelo's nearby work shed to the piazza.

2. FALSE Actually, playing games with small marbles was popular in Egypt, Greece, and Rome hundreds of years before Michelangelo was born.

3. b Michelangelo and Leonardo da Vinci never got along very well. They agreed to the city's challenge to paint large battle scenes on opposite walls of the Grand Council Hall in Florence. Unfortunately, neither artist finished his painting.

4. b Michelangelo was determined to learn all he could about the human body. He was given permission to dissect, examine, and sketch bodies at a hospital morgue in Florence. Michelangelo's scientific studies are one reason his figures have such an amazing lifelike look.

5. c Between 1980 and 1989, art restorers used a special solution applied with a brush and carefully removed with a sponge soaked in pure water. It wasn't easy to remove years of smoky soot from church candles and pollution from car exhaust. When the job was finished, people were surprised by how many bright colors Michelangelo used in his painting.

6. c Anchovies, tortellini, salami, spinach and bread were a few of Michelangelo's favorite foods. Amazingly, Michelangelo's actual grocery lists exist! He would often draw pictures of food items he wanted because the assistants he sent to the market didn't know how to read.